# Illustrated Children's Books

JOHN BARR

## The British Library

Published by
The British Library,
Great Russell Street,
London WC1B 3DG

and 27 South Main Street,
Wolfeboro, New Hampshire
03894–2069

BL British Library
Cataloguing in Publication Data

Barr, John, 1934–
  Illustrated children's books.
  I. Illustrated books,
  Childrens—
  2. Illustration of books—19th
  century
  3. Illustration of books—20th
  century
  I. Title  II. British Library
  741.64'2'09034  NC965

  ISBN 0–7123–0098–8

Library of Congress Cataloging
in Publication Data

Barr, John, 1934–
  Illustrated children's books.
  Bibliography: p.
  1. Illustrated books,
  Children's—Library
  resources—England—
  London.  2. Illustrated books,
  Children's—Publishing—
  Great Britain—History.
  3. Picture-books for children—
  Bibliography.
  4. Illustrated books,
  Children's—Bibliography.
  5. British Library.  I. Title.
  Z1037.B277  1986
  [PN1009.A1]  016.8088'09282
  86–21618
  ISBN 0–7123–0098–8 (pbk.)

Designed by Roger Davies
Typeset in Monophoto Ehrhardt
by August Filmsetting, Haydock,
St. Helens
Origination by York House
Graphics, Hanwell
Printed in England by Jolly and
Barber Ltd., Rugby

*Acknowledgements*

The author and publishers
are grateful to the following
for permission to reproduce
illustrations in this book:
The Bodley Head; George G.
Harrap Ltd; Hodder and
Stoughton Ltd; Houghton
Mifflin; Penguin Books, Ltd;
The Estate of J.C. Robinson.

*Front cover*: Bret Harte: *The
Queen of the Pirate Isle . . .
Illustrated by Kate
Greenaway. Engraved and
printed by Edmund Evans.*
Chatto & Windus, 1886.
[12811.h.21]

*Back cover*: 'Modern and
functional [English]
children's clothes'. Engraving
in *Journal des Luxus und der
Moden (Weimar)*. Bd.2,
1787.
[P.P.5227]

*Title-page*: Adapted from *An
Alphabetical Arrangement of
Animals for Little Naturalists
by Sally Sketch*. Harris &
Son, 1821
[7207.a.11]

# Contents

# Introduction

Children's books – however the term is defined – have from the outset contained pictures for the instruction or diversion of young readers.

In the first decades of the 19th century, and again in those leading up to the First World War, the illustration of British children's books attained a remarkable level of technical and artistic excellence.

A special attraction of 19th-century and earlier books lies in the fact that the illustrations are original graphics in the modern sense, because only towards the end of the century did the processes of photomechanical reproduction come into general use. Before that the artist's drawing was transferred by a professional craftsman, or by the artist himself, onto the block or plate for printing. The printing was done from a wood block (in relief or 'letterpress' printing), from the grooves, furrows and dots on a metal plate, or from the inked surface of a lithographic stone.

The acquisition by copyright deposit of the productions of British publishers, which became effective from the mid-19th century onwards, has ensured that the British Museum (and since 1973, the British Library) has built up one of the largest collections of children's books in the world. It comprises a very wide-ranging, though incomplete, archive for the Victorian period and later. Many older books for children, some of them rare or unique, have also been acquired, usually by purchase or donation.

This book describes and reproduces a selection of the interesting, beautiful and amusing illustrations in children's books published down to the 1920s. It also gives a brief account of some of the outstanding artists, publishers, and printers (not all of them British) who made them, and how they worked.

All the books illustrated were published in London, unless otherwise stated.

*Left*: E. Boyd Smith. *The Story of Noah's Ark*. (See page 78.)

# Techniques of reproduction

All illustrators are affected by the methods used to reproduce their work. Between about 1780 and 1920 new processes were developed and used in the production of illustrations in books, each with its own strengths and limitations. On the whole artists have been successful only when they have taken into account the distinctive qualities of these processes and modified their drawing and colour accordingly.

Either woodcuts, or and in the more expensive volumes, copper engravings printed on a separate press, were used for the illustration of children's books until the development of wood engraving at the end of the 18th century by Thomas Bewick. 'In metal engraving you cut ditches, fill them with ink and press your paper into them; and in wood engraving you leave ridges, rub the tops of them with ink and press them on your paper', explained John Ruskin (*Ariadne Florentina*, sec. 76).

## Woodcuts

A woodcut is made with a knife and gouges on the soft or plank side of a wood block. The surface is cut away to leave only the design (in reverse) that is to be printed in relief. This remaining surface is then inked and impressions taken from it. (See 3, 7).

## Copper engraving

The design is cut (again in reverse) with a burin or engraving tool into the surface of a copper plate. The plate is inked and wiped clean so that only the engraved furrows hold ink. The plate is then put into a press with a sheet of dampened paper, which under pressure draws out the ink and prints the design. Copper engravings allowed for finer detail than woodcuts but they had to be printed on a separate press from the text. (See 1, 2.)

## Etching

A metal plate, usually copper, is covered with a ground of blackened wax and the design is scratched directly through the ground, exposing the copper. The plate is then immersed in acid and the exposed metal is eaten away or 'bitten' by the acid to produce lines and dots. When the lines to be printed lightest have bitten furrows of the required depth, these lines are 'stopped out' with acid-resisting varnish. The immersion is repeated until the darker lines have bitten sufficiently deep. The etched lines on the plate can also be gone over with a burin to get lines of varying width and depth. As in copper engraving the surface is wiped clean and the design is printed from the inked furrows. (See 16, 18.)

## Stipple engraving

The engraver builds up a mass of dots, not directly on the plate, but on the wax etching ground, so as to print in grainy areas of tone. (See 14.)

## Steel engraving

Copper plates were expensive and wore out quickly. Etching on steel was established as a practical working method about 1824, with the advantage that a long print-run could be taken from the plate. (See 6.)

## Lithography

In 1788–89 Alois Senefelder, who wanted a cheap way to duplicate his scripts for plays, invented lithography, a reproductive method based on the fact that grease and water do not mix; it was not, however, extensively used for illustration until after the Napoleonic wars. In lithography the design is drawn in some greasy substance on a slab of limestone. When the stone is dampened the water settles only on the un-marked, non-greasy areas. The stone is then inked by a roller with greasy printer's ink which can stick to the greasy, marked areas only, because the water repels it elsewhere. The design is then printed by running the paper and the inked, dampened stone together through a flat-bed press. A light sheet of grained aluminium or zinc was later substituted for the unwieldy stone. The flexible metal could be wrapped around the cylinder of a rotary press.

Lithography, like etching, has the advantage of requiring no re-working of the artist's drawing by another hand or in another medium. He has the same freedom to make broad or fine strokes with pen, brush or pencil as he has working directly on paper, with a full range of tone from dark to pale.

The first lithographs were black and white, but colour was sometimes added by hand. The application of lithography to colour printing (chromolithography), an elaborate process patented in 1837, required up to twenty separate drawings and stones – one for each of the colours, which were printed in succession. (See **40**.)

## Wood engraving

In woodcuts the artist's design is cut in relief along the grain of a plank. In Bewick's wood-engraving, however, the design is cut, usually in delicate white lines on black, into the closely packed fibres of the end-grain of box-wood, using an engraving tool or burin.

Thomas Bewick engraved his own designs in pin-prick and hair-line detail on box-wood blocks that could print thousands of impressions before showing signs of wear. Bewick also engraved other artist's designs, and, by the mid-19th century, what he sometimes did had become the regular practice. The growing popular market for books and periodicals required copious illustration produced at speed; wood-engraving was pressed into service to meet this demand. Artists handed their drawings to professional engravers who cut them on wood blocks strong enough to withstand long print-runs on the new steam-driven presses. A common time-saving device was to draw directly on the wood, or on paper that was then pasted on to the block.

Bewick cut lines in the wood block with a burin as if he were engraving a metal plate; it was, however, printed in relief – that is, the ink was rolled on to the surface only, from which impressions were taken, reproducing the original design in white lines on a black background. The reproductive wood engravers usually retained the *line* of a design on the block and dug out all the surrounding white space from the block.

It was difficult to transfer with complete accuracy the varying weight, thickness and texture of the artist's lines on to the block. Artists often made drawings in wash, chalk and pencil in which the attempt to design for the distinctive capabilities of wood engraving was largely abandoned.

The original wood blocks were irreplaceable and so from about 1830 onwards stereotypes and electrotypes in metal were made to duplicate them. These could stand up to even longer print-runs.

Once drawings could be transferred on to the block photographically (a process introduced about 1868), they could be enlarged or reduced in size, and imposed in a reverse image on the block.

In the 1860s the leading firms of wood engravers – the Dalziel brothers, Joseph Swain and Edmund Evans – not only maintained high levels of competence and craftsmanship, but branched out into publishing themselves. They commissioned illustrations for their own publications, or for books issued by other publishers, from the leading illustrators of the day.

## Colour printing

Hand-colouring increased the cost of illustration, and books containing hand-coloured plates generally cost half as much again as uncoloured copies. George Baxter in 1835 patented his method of colour printing, in which he used a metal plate (usually engraved) as a key to print dark outlines and shaded areas of tone in a neutral tint, and added colours in succession from a series of wood blocks. Different inks were needed for printing from metal and from wood. Baxter ground his own inks, engraved his own plates and blocks and did his own printing. Not surprisingly his process was generally too costly for book-work, but in 1850 it was modified and used under licence by Joseph Martin Kronheim and his successors, at first only for frontispieces (See **41**).

Tinted wood-engraving was developed at about the same time as colour lithography. Baxter pointed the way to a simpler method of colour illustration from wood blocks which was developed by Edmund Evans, the skilled and sensitive craftsman who printed the children's picture books of Walter Crane, Kate Greenaway and Randolph Caldecott.

## Line-blocks

In photomechanical or 'process' engraving, the camera lens replaced the craftsman's hand and eye. Sir Joseph Wilson Swan (who later invented the incandescent light-bulb) in 1864 patented the earliest process based on the discovery that bichromated gelatine hardens when exposed to light.

A zinc plate coated with light-sensitive emulsion is exposed to light under a photographic negative of the artist's drawing. The light hardens the emulsion under the transparent parts only of the negative, that is, the lines of the drawing. The soft, unexposed emulsion is then washed off the plate. The hardened lines of the photographic image are dusted with powdered resin, which under heat forms a 'resist', and when the plate is etched in acid the lines remain in relief. The etched plate, mounted on a block 'type-high', is called a line-block and can be printed together with the type-set text (see **56**, **58**).

The line-block became commercially viable in the 1880s, and by the

1890s Aubrey Beardsley and other artists were making drawings in solid blacks balanced by large areas of white and spidery lines, with no attempt to render tone, light and shade, or modelling. The line-block could reproduce lines, dots and blocks of uniform tone – black and white, for example, but not shades of grey. (For this a half-tone block is needed.)

## Half-tone

Half-tone engraving made possible the accurate reproduction of gradations of tone. In this process a finely ruled glass screen breaks down a tonal image into a pattern of tiny dots invisible to the naked eye. The original image is photographed through the screen, producing on the negative a myriad of equally spaced dots at the intersections of the lines. The dots, which cover the whole printing area, vary in size; for the darker tones they are large and run together. The process thus depends on an optical illusion, similar to that by which we see the lines on a television screen as a continuous tonal image. The resulting negative of tiny dots is printed on a sensitized metal plate, which, like the line-block, is then prepared by etching for printing.

Line-blocks could be printed together with type-set text on the same paper, but there was a drawback with half-tone. Accurate reproduction of tone required a very fine mesh of lines on the screen. The resulting dots, however, were so tiny that they could only be printed clearly on an absolutely smooth surface. Half-tone plates had therefore to be printed separately from the text of the book on specially coated glossy paper.

## Half-tone colour printing

Colour printing in photomechanical processes is based on Newton's discovery that coloured light is composed of the three primary colours (red, yellow, blue). By about 1895 the half-tone process became commercially available. By means of glass filters each primary colour in the artist's original is in turn photographed and transferred to a half-tone plate. Each of the three resulting plates is then printed in succession, in ink of the appropriate colour, so that the superimposed images reproduce the colours of the original, (See 36, 65). A fourth plate (black, to strengthen the shadows and deepen tone) became general in printing in the 1920s.

## Offset photolithography

In offset photolithography the image (illustration *and* text) is photographed onto a flexible metal plate which is then wrapped around the cylinder of a rotary press. This plate, however, does not touch the paper but prints the design onto a rubber-covered roller, which in turn prints it onto the paper. Because of the suppleness of the rubber and its sensitivity to pressure, ordinary paper can receive an adequate impression and there is no need for specially-coated paper. Most illustrated children's books today are printed by this method.

# Early children's books

## Comenius

The first picture book for children, the *Orbis sensualium pictus* or 'Visible World', by the Czech educational reformer Comenius, was published in Nuremberg in 1658 and illustrated with 150 different woodcuts. Comenius sought to impart to children in simple language information and ideas about the world around them and to teach them Latin by the direct method. 'Pictures are the most intelligible books that children can look upon', he wrote. The pictures were essential to his purpose because, Comenius believed, only when something has been grasped by the senses can language begin to explain it further.

There soon appeared an English translation (1659) of *Orbis pictus* by a school-master, Charles Hoole, for which the woodcuts were re-drawn and

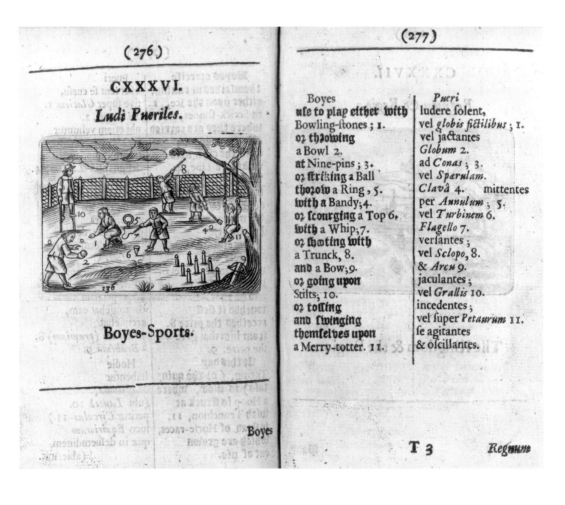

*Little Goody Two-Shoes.*

1 Comenius *Orbis sensualium pictus ... Visible world ... Translated into English, by Charles Hoole ... for the use of young Latine-Scholars.* J. Kirton, 1659.
[E.2116 (1.)]

2 *The History of Little Goody Two-Shoes.*
J. Newbery, 1765
[C.180.a.3]
The only known copy of the first edition. Reproduced to original size.

engraved on copper plates, resulting in greater precision and detail (1). The engraved plates, unlike woodcuts, had to be printed on a separate press from the text, and Hoole in his preface mentions the 'dearnesse of the book by reason of brasse cuts in it'.

Each object in the plate is numbered, and the Latin and English names are given in the text, sometimes with a brief explanation. The picture-subjects range from natural history and trades such as carpentry and tailoring to such topics as 'Moral Philosophy' and 'The society betwixt Parents and Children'. Warfare and judicial punishment are not avoided; but we are also shown a stage-play, conjurors, dice, chess and tennis and other games. In the *Orbis pictus*, as in most didactic books for children over the next century, entertainment took second place, supplied only to sugar the pill of learning. In 1744, however, two works were published in English solely for children's pleasure and diversion.

## Tommy Thumb's Pretty Song Book

One of them was *Tommy Thumb's Pretty Song Book*: no copy of Vol. I is known and the British Library's copy of Vol. II is the only one extant (4). The text and illustrations were printed from engraved plates throughout, on facing pages alternately in red and black. The publisher, Mrs Mary Cooper, also published music, in which the words were printed from letters stamped into the plate. The song-book is the earliest printed collection of thirty-nine traditional nursery rhymes, 'Bah Bah, a Black Sheep', 'Who did kill Cock Robin', 'Oranges and lemons' and 'London Bridge is falling down'. Nothing is known about how they were collected,

*The little m Play.*

LEAP-FROG.

THIS ſtoops down his Head,
　　Whilſt that ſprings up high;
But then you will find,
　　He'll ſtoop by and by.

MORAL,

Juſt ſo 'tis at Court;
　　To-day you're in *Place*;
To morrow, perhaps,
　　You're quite in Diſgrace.

BIRDS-

*The great N Play.*

BIRDS-NESTING.

HERE two naughty Boys,
　　Hard-hearted in Jeſt,
Deprive a poor *Bird*
Of her young and her Neſt.

MORAL.

Thus Men, out of Joke,
　　(Be't ſpoke to their Shame)
Too often make free
　　With others good Name.

TRAIN-

3 *A little pretty pocket book,
intended for the instruction and
amusement of little Master
Tommy and pretty Miss
Polly . . . Tenth edition.*
J. Newbery, 1760
[Ch.760/6]

though the editor, 'N. Lovechild', may have been Mary Cooper herself.

Mary Cooper had in 1743 brought out (and probably compiled) *The Child's new play-thing*, a spelling and reading book using traditional rhymes and shortened versions of mediaeval tales – such as Guy of Warwick, Reynard the Fox and St George. These rhymes and tales became familiar to 18th-century children in the inexpensive chapbooks sold by pedlars, in which woodcuts of little artistic worth, often originally made for quite different texts, were frequently re-used.

## John Newbery

Of the other innovative book for children published in 1744 no copy survives: 'This day is published', wrote the *Penny Morning Advertiser* for 18 June, '*A Little Pretty Pocket Book*'. The earliest surviving edition is the tenth of 1760, and the British Library's copy is the only one extant (3).

*A Little Pretty Pocket Book* is based on the school primer and the greater part is an alphabet of upper- and lower-case letters, illustrated, with no particular relevance, by rough woodcuts of solemn little boys in adult costume playing cricket, hop-scotch, baseball and other games; there is a verse and an unrelated moral underneath each woodcut. Girls join the

**4** *Tommy Thumb's Pretty Song Book*. Vol. II. Mary Cooper, [1744]
[C.59.a.20]
No copy of Vol. I is known, and this copy of Vol. II is unique.

boys in the next section which shows two children saying their prayers, asking a blessing of their parents, reading and giving money to those less fortunate than themselves.

*A Little Pretty Pocket Book* is one of nearly 400 titles published between 1744 and the end of the century by the firm founded by John Newbery; of these the British Library holds about 170. Perhaps the most famous of them is *The History of Little Goody Two-Shoes* (1765) (2), of which the only known copy of the first edition was acquired by the British Library in 1965. *Goody Two-Shoes*, which has been ascribed to Oliver Goldsmith and, more probably, to John Newbery himself, is the earliest sustained piece of original fiction published for children in English. In the story, an orphan, Marjorie, later known as Goody Two-Shoes, by extraordinary industry makes her career as an itinerant teacher or 'trotting tutoress'. The narrative is diffuse and anecdotal, and illustrated by postage-stamp-sized woodcuts. The title page, however, is engraved. Nearly 200 editions published in both England and America attest the popularity of *Goody Two-Shoes* over the next century.

Newbery certainly did not 'invent' children's books, nor even start a fashion for them; but it was he who first promoted them as an important branch of publishing.

## 'Robinson Crusoe'

Three of the greatest children's classics – Bunyans' *Pilgrim's Progress*, Swift's *Gulliver's Travels* and Defoe's *Robinson Crusoe* – were not originally intended by their authors for children, but have since been taken over by them. Publishers have brought out countless editions, usually abridged and illustrated, for young readers. In the early chapbook editions woodcuts emphasized important moments or features of the narrative and helped bridge the gaps between the cut-down and the complete texts.

*Robinson Crusoe* has, since its first appearance in 1719, remained perennially popular with children and adults alike and provided a model for many similar stories of survival in primitive conditions. Defoe presented his fiction as a true story and based it on contemporary accounts of Alexander Selkirk's five-year sojourn on an uninhabited island. The frontispiece of the first edition, engraved by John Pine (5) fixed an instantly recognizable image of the castaway which has remained scarcely unaltered for generations of readers and illustrators (6) – including stage-designers and caricaturists. It follows Defoe's detailed description of his hero, with the omission of his goat-skin umbrella and the saw and hatchet in his belt. Crusoe's excessive weaponry and heavy home-made garments have recently been seen as a representation of European domination over a tropical environment and its unclothed inhabitants. They are certainly warranted

5 *The Life and Strange Surprizing Adventures of Robinson Crusoe, of York, Mariner ... Written by himself.* W. Taylor, 1719
[C.30.f.6]

**6 George Cruikshank.**
Daniel Defoe *The life and
surprising adventures of
Robinson Crusoe ... Illustrated
with engravings from drawings
by G. Cruikshank.* 2 vols.
John Major, 1831
[635.g.20]

by the text, together with the indispensable equipment that Crusoe salvaged by raft from the ship-wreck. This is shown in an unusually vigorous and clearly printed woodcut in a late (about 1840) chapbook edition (7).

## Thomas Bewick

In 1767 Bewick, at the age of fourteen, was apprenticed to a Newcastle metal engraver, Ralph Beilby, whose partner he later became. As well as engraving bank-notes, door-plates, arms and initials on metal, Bewick also cut wood blocks for tickets, bill-headings and decorative inserts for jobbing printers, and for illustrations in chapbooks. Bewick eventually became famous for the finely observed and exquisitely executed wood engravings in the volumes of natural history that he wrote and published himself: *Quadrupeds* (1790) and *British Birds* (1797, 1804). The vignettes and tail-pieces recall the scenes of his Tyneside boyhood, with children scampering among grave-stones, sailing toy boats, playing soldiers and teasing dogs.

Bewick's illustrations for his early fable edition of 1784 and for the *Aesop* of 1818 (**9, 10, 11,**) were closely modelled both in design and technique on the illustrations of Elisha Kirkall – 'white-line' engravings in relief on soft metal (probably type-metal) which had appeared in successive editions of Samuel Croxall's *Aesop* since 1722. 'I was always

7 *The life and wonderful adventures of Robinson Crusoe.* Glasgow: Francis Orr, [1840] [Ch.401.d.79] A woodcut in a late chapbook edition.

extremely fond of that book', wrote Bewick. Most of Kirkall's designs were in turn derived from the etchings with which Francis Barlow illustrated his *Fables* (1666). Bewick, Kirkall and Barlow all depict Aesop's animals, not anthropomorphically but naturally, in fields, forests, and streams.

Bewick's importance lies not only in the beauty and freshness of his designs and the delicate effects he obtained, but in his development of wood-engraving as a medium for book illustration.

## John Harris

The cheerful little illustrated books published for children at the beginning of the 19th century by John Harris, Benjamin Tabart, William Godwin, John Marshall and others show a great technical advance on nearly all their predecessors. They were usually printed on one side of the paper only, with the illustrations at the top of the page and a short text underneath, which was often engraved rather than set up in type. John Harris stands out among his rivals both for his taste and his enterprise. He used engravings on wood and metal and later lithographs, both plain and coloured, to adorn nursery rhymes, puzzles, pence and multiplication tables, grammars and natural history.

In 1801 Harris took over the publishing business, largely juvenile, of Mrs Elizabeth Newbery, for whom he had acted as manager. In 1805 he brought out an anonymous little book of funny verses with no didactic element whatsoever: *The Comic Adventures of Mother Hubbard and her*

8 Anon. *Home and foreign birds. A book for young children.* G. Routledge, 1856 [12807.b.16] *Far left:* Corncrake. *Left:* Snipe.

**9, 10, 11 Thomas Bewick.**
*The Fables of Aesop, and
others, with designs on wood by
T. Bewick.* Newcastle:
T. Bewick & Son, 1818
[Ch.810/123]
'As instruction is of little
avail without constant
cheerfulness and occasional
amusement,' Bewick tells us,
he also provided, in addition
to a framed illustration at the
head of each fable, delightful
tail-pieces 'of gaiety and
humour' which provide an
alternative comment. *Top*:
The dog and his shadow.
*Centre*: The angler and the
little fish.
*Bottom*: Tailpiece to 'The
Angler and the little fish'.

*dog: illustrated with fifteen elegant engravings on copper plate.*
The dedication reads:

'To J— B— Esq^r M.P. County of—at whose suggestion and at whose House these notable sketches were design'd, this Volume is with all suitable deference Dedicated by his Humble Servant S.C.M.'

The amateur artist who supplied the sketches for the engravings, together with the verses, was a well-connected young lady, Sarah Catherine Martin. While her father was naval commissioner at Portsmouth, Prince William Henry who was stationed there in 1785–6 offered to marry her; but Sarah, then aged seventeen, declined. The Prince later ascended the throne as King William IV; Sarah never married. When she and her sister Judith were staying at the home of John Pollexfen Bastard, the member of Parliament of the dedication, it was to Judith that their host was attracted. He (understandably) found Sarah's incessant talking annoying and encouraged her to entertain herself; *Mother Hubbard* was the result. The dedication, with its veiled suggestion of political satire, helped to turn the old nursery rhyme into a fashionable best-seller, and within a few months 10,000 copies had been sold, at a shilling a copy. Text and illustrations were printed together from copper plates; for the second edition (1806) (**12**) the plates were re-engraved.

*Mother Hubbard* set the tone for similar well-printed, light-hearted booklets in square format with pretty illustrations. To nurseries and classrooms, up till then furnished with books of moral tales and potted facts, adorned at best by an engraved frontispiece or woodcuts of varying quality, they brought style and colour.

Harris's next success was *The Butterfly's Ball* (1807), an anonymous poem for children written, (as rumour – correctly – had it) by another M.P., the historian and banker William Roscoe, and illustrated by William Mulready. In 1819 Harris, now joined in the business by his son, increased the size of his little books so that the illustrations could fit comfortably on the page with typeset text.

Until the 1830s colour in book illustrations was applied by hand. Like the sheets of cut-out characters and scenery then printed for toy theatres – 'penny plain and twopence coloured' – John Harris's books and those of his competitors were available either uncoloured, to be coloured later by the purchaser, or (at a much higher price) already coloured, usually by production-lines of children, following a model and sometimes using stencils. Each colourist supplied one colour on the printed sheet as required and passed it on for the next.

Artists were now expected to draw designs in firm outline which could easily be filled with broad areas of flat colour, using a minimum of detail and shading and almost blank backgrounds. The colourists' skill, combined with good draughtsmanship, conferred on these simple illustrations something of the sparkle and gaiety of the Regency.

Such books, especially the coloured copies, were beyond the means of all but the well-to-do. The stories and verses in them are mostly about the well-fed, well-dressed offspring of prosperous families, living in fine

Old Mother Hubbard
Went to the Cupboard,
 To give the poor Dog a bone,
When she came there
 The Cupboard was bare,
And so the poor Dog had none.

She went to the Bakers
 To buy him some bread;
When she came back
 The Dog was dead!

**12** [Sarah Catherine Martin]
*The comic adventures of Old
Mother Hubbard and her dog.*
(Second edition.) John
Harris, 1806
[Ch.800/101 (4.)]

houses with toys and pets, books and governesses. The poor make brief appearances as the objects of charity (**14**) and a means of self-improvement for the more fortunate. On the other hand, the Quaker publisher and engraver William Darton introduced such topical themes as the anti-slavery cause (**15**) to his juvenile list.

## George Cruikshank

George Cruikshank was the first important artist to make his living exclusively by illustrating books. During the Regency period Cruikshank had been a leading caricaturist, but when the market for political and social satire declined he turned to books. Cruikshank's vast output of illustrations, produced over sixty years for every purpose and age-group, evolved from caricature. 'He was at his best' writes Ruari McLean, 'where drama, mystery, horror or excitement were required. Probably no other illustrator has ever made so many pictures that haunt the memory . . . even if the context is unknown or forgotten'.

Cruikshank often engraved his own designs himself, whether on metal or on wood. In his *Robinson Crusoe* volume, for instance, the frontispiece (**6**), which shows Crusoe in goatskin hat and leggings and armed with gun and axe receiving Friday's submission, is 'etched on steel', while the other illustrations are small wood engravings, strong on domestic detail. As a result, even when Cruikshank made drawings for professional engravers, he suited his style to what they could accomplish, so that the difference between his drawing and the printed result is negligible. Etching, however, was the medium in which Cruikshank excelled, though one seldom used by later artists in children's books.

# A a
## Angry Alice

'Tis pictur'd here in Angry Alice;
The mischiefs which arise from malice.

# V v
## Vain Valentine

There's none I trust that will incline
To be as vain as Valentine.

But what a picture here is given?!
O Charity, meek child of Heaven?!
May all the rich thy virtues feel?,
And learn this lesson at each meal;
To clothe the naked, feed the poor,
Nor drive the beggar from their door.

Plate 3

THE

# BLACK MAN'S LAMENT.

THE PETITION FOR ABOLISHING THE SLAVE-TRADE.

———

COME, listen to my plaintive ditty,
 Ye tender hearts, and children dear!
And, should it move your souls to pity,
 Oh! try to *end* the griefs you hear.

SUGAR-CANE.

———

There is a *beauteous plant* \*, that grows
 In western India's sultry clime,
Which makes, alas! the Black man's woes,
 And also makes the White man's crime.

———

\* " A field of canes, when standing in the month of November, when it is in arrow or full blossom, (says Beckford, in his descriptive account of the Island of Jamaica,) is one of the most beautiful productions that the pen or pencil can possibly describe. It, in common, rises from three to eight feet, or more, in height; a difference

**17 George Cruikshank.** [John Ayrton Paris] *Philosophy in sport made Science in earnest . . . by the aid of popular toys and sports.* Vol. 1. Longman [etc.], 1827
1136.f.17]
Longmans paid Cruikshank £30 for 25 small wood engravings.

**18 George Cruikshank.**
*Cinderella* D. Bogue, [1854].
(George Cruikshank's Fairy Library)
[C.70.b.9]
Etchings.

**16 George Cruikshank.** [J. & W.] Grimm *German popular stories.*
C. Baldwyn, 1823
[Cup.402.b.18]
Cruikshank's etched title-page vignette reminds us that these tales were meant for family amusement.

The Pumpkin, and the Rat, and the mice, and the Lizards, being changed by the Fairy, into a
Coach, Horses, and Servants, to take Cinderella to the Ball at the Royal Palace

Designed & Etched

by George Cruikshank

The Fairy changing Cinderella's Kitchen dress, into a beautiful Ball dress !!!

CONJUNCTION

*and, but, if, yet,*

CONJUNCTIONS *are words that join sentences and words together, you and I rode together but we did not reach London, yet we saw it.— and, but, yet are all conjunctions*

INTERJECTIONS

*ah! alas! O! la! fie! hush! behold!*

*O dear!*

*Ah! my Brother*

*my Sister!*

*Alas!*

INTERJECTIONS *are exclamations denoting any sudden emotion of the mind, either of pain, pleasure, or surprise.*

In the stories from German folklore collected and recorded by the scholars Jacob and Wilhelm Grimm, the traditional fairy tale gained a new and lasting currency. The first German editions (1812, 1815) contained a long introduction and notes – but no pictures. Edgar Taylor, however, the London lawyer who translated the tales for the first English edition 'had the amusement of some young friends principally in view', as he wrote in a letter to the Grimm brothers. The result, *German popular stories* (1823, 26) was adorned with a frontispiece (16) and eleven small etchings, each no more than two inches square, by Cruikshank, which were greatly admired by the Grimms (and later, by Thackeray and Ruskin).

In 1853 Cruikshank began his 'Fairy Library', a series of traditional fairy tales for which he provided the text as well as the illustrations. He had by then become an enthusiastic teetotaller. In *Cinderella* the King proclaims that to celebrate his son's wedding 'there shall be no more fountains of wine in my dominions'. This 'moralizing' of traditional tales provoked an attack from Cruikshank's friend Dickens in the essay 'Frauds against the fairies', which effectively killed the series as a publishing venture. The lively etchings nevertheless remain among the finest fairy tale illustrations (18).

ENSIGN SEMICOLON, marked thus;

See, how Semicolon is strutting with pride;
Into two or more parts he'll a sentence divide.
As "John's a good scholar; but George is a better:
"One wrote a fair copy; the other a letter."
Without this gay ensign we little could do;
And when he appears we must pause & count TWO.

19 (*Opposite*): *The Paths of Learning Strewed with Flowers, or English Grammar Illustrated.* Harris & Son, 1820

[Ch.820/30]

ROBERT'S first interview with Mr. STOPS.

Young Robert, could read, but he gabbled so fast;
And ran on with such speed, that all meaning he lost.
Till one Morning he met Mr. Stops, by the way,
Who advis'd him to listen to what he should say.
Then, ent'ring the house, he a riddle repeated,
To shew, WITHOUT STOPS, how the ear may be cheated.

20 *Punctuation personified: or, pointing made easy, by Mr. Stops.* J. Harris, 1824

[12804.ee.12]

3

So of a piece of willow bark,
A boat he soon did make,
And having stored it well with nut
He launched it on the lake,
Tho' his Father, and his Mother,
Both begg'd that he would stay,
He spread his tail, to catch the gal
And boldly sailed away.

**21** *The Travels of Bob the Squirrel.* J. Bysh, [1840] [012806.ee.35 (18.)] The text was engraved on wood with the illustrations.

For two long days, and two long nights,
He gaily on did float,
But on the third a storm arose,
And sunk his little boat.
All drench'd, and cold, and weary,
He struggled with the tide,
Till almost gone, with swimming on,
He reached the farther side.

**22** *The wonderful tour of Little Peter Paganini.* Dean & Munday, [1841] [838.f.26 (13.)]

Young Pag took the Fiddle, and went, for a stare,
To the British Museum near Bloomsbury Square;
Here some looked wise, some grave, some glum,
Says Pag, 'tis to make you all merry I've come.
He played them a tune, they danced from their Books,
And delighted each seemed, if we judge by their looks.

# Nonsense and fantasy

## Edward Lear

Edward Lear was a painter of topographical and natural history subjects. He made his name with drawings of parrots, superbly reproduced in lithography by Hullmandel (1830–32), and hand-coloured. Lear's *Book of Nonsense*, (**23**), composed to amuse the children of his patron, the Earl of Derby, was published in 1846 by Thomas McLean, a firm of print-sellers who brought out topographical views, among them Lear's. McLean issued the limericks and striking little drawings of *The Book of Nonsense* in two small volumes of lithographs traced from Lear's drawings. They became popular in upper-class households, but it was not until fifteen years later, when *The Book of Nonsense* was revised, re-drawn and expanded that a

**23 Edward Lear.** *A Book of nonsense.* (By Derry Down Derry). Thos. McLean, 1846 [C.117.a.60]
The first edition of Lear's first *Book of nonsense* appeared in two parts, each consisting of thirty-six lithographed plates of drawings and text. Both have this lithographed design on the upper cover.

**24 Edward Lear.** *A Book of nonsense* Frederick Warne, [1875?] [12332.dd.21]
Title-page; coloured wood engraving.

There was an Old Derry down Derry, who loved to see little folks merry;
So he made them a Book, and with laughter they shook
At the fun of that Derry down Derry.

trade edition by Routledge, Warne, who specialized in children's books, became a best-seller. This and subsequent editions, including those printed in colour (24), were illustrated by wood-engravings made by the Dalziel brothers.

Lear deliberately adopted a childishly naïve style. He enlarged the heads of his figures so as to emphasize facial expressions, and disposed their limbs in gestures of astonishment or helplessness. They are a child's-eye view of his professional work. The birds and animals in the Earl's private menagerie reappear in his nonsense books and the drawings do not lose their basis in natural history, even though the verses (which he made up while he was drawing) do. Each is a specimen, perching, nesting or strutting about like the parrots and toucans that Lear drew for a living.

## 'Struwwelpeter'

In December 1844 Dr Heinrich Hoffmann of Frankfurt bought a blank exercise-book for his four-year-old son: 'I went to town to buy a picture-book for him as a present, but what did I find? Long tales, stupid collections of pictures, moralizing stories, beginning and ending with admonitions like "The good child must be truthful" or "children must keep clean". etc'. So Dr Hoffmann filled the exercise-book with his own 'jolly tales and funny pictures', in the style he had already evolved to amuse his child-patients.

When in the following year Dr Hoffmann was persuaded to publish his drawings and verses, he supervised not only the lithographer who transferred his drawings on to the stone but also the women who coloured them by hand. In successive editions (eventually entitled *Struwwelpeter*) Hoffmann's original wispy figures were filled out and the settings became more elaborate; but the poses, gestures and simple outlines of each character remain unchanged. (26, 27.)

The grotesque exaggerations of *Struwwelpeter* parody current cautionary tales. It is ironical that this 'spoof', by a doctor who later ran one of the most enlightened mental hospitals of his day, has been considered by some psychiatrists to be harmful to children. *Struwwelpeter* has in its turn inspired countless parodies. The First World War evoked *Swollen-headed William* (1914), in which E.V. Lucas, who wrote and edited numerous children's books, described Kaiser Wilhelm's ambitions in terms of *Struwwelpeter*. But neither this, nor *Struwwelhitler* (1941) by 'Dr Schrecklichkeit', was meant for children. The *Egyptian Struwwelpeter* (1899) (30), however, is the English version of an entertainment devised by children – the three children of a Viennese doctor, for a family friend. Their 'Ur-Struwwelpeter' was, like Dr Hoffmann's, originally intended as a present with no thought of publication. Supposedly found in the desert sands on a papyrus, the verses were written, not in an exercise-book, but on sheets of brown paper on the kitchen table. One of the children drew convincing copies of Egyptian antiquities in the Kunsthistorisches Museum, and another wrote a pseudo-scientific introduction. The *Egyptian Struwwelpeter* apparently encouraged other archaeological 'finds', such as Dean &

Son's *Old Nursery Rhymes dug up at the Pyramids* (1902), bound in sack-cloth with a ribbon and a seal.

## Richard Doyle

As a boy Richard Doyle developed a talent for drawing comic borders, fanciful initials and imaginative head- and tail-pieces. He became, like his father, an illustrator for *Punch*, and designed their famous cover. In 1850, however, Doyle resigned in protest against the paper's anti-Catholic articles (to be replaced by John Tenniel). He then turned to illustrating fairy-tales. For many Victorians fairy-land and the spirit-world held a fascination similar to that exerted today by the aliens and extra-terrestrials of science-fiction. Doyle's delicately drawn fairies, with their clear porcelain colourings, fed this fashionable appetite. But he was also capable of more robust subjects (31). His heir and nephew, Sir Arthur Conan Doyle, modelled some features of Sherlock Holmes (his violin-playing, his pride of ancestry) on his uncle.

## 'Alice in Wonderland'

The publication in 1865 of *Alice in Wonderland* marks the complete emancipation of children's books from didactic and moralizing constraints. There is no preaching; indeed, earlier edifying verse for children is parodied in versions now better known than the originals. Children, whether Alice herself or the young readers, are neither patronised nor sentimentalised. As W.H. Auden pointed out, 'It is the child-heroine Alice who is invariably reasonable, self-controlled and polite, while all the other inhabitants, human or animal, of Wonderland and the Looking-Glass are unsocial eccentrics – at the mercy of their passions and extremely bad

**25 Richard Doyle.** *An old fairy tale ('The Sleeping Beauty') told anew in pictures and verse by R. Doyle and J.R. Planché. The pictures engraved by the brothers Dalziel.* [London,] 1865
[11650.f.10]
Doyle's illustrations for 'The Sleeping Beauty' were commissioned by the Dalziels and took him fifteen years to complete. The wide-eyed nymphets and leering elves were drawn with a fine quill pen, as Doyle found difficulty in drawing with pencil on the wood-block.

And see! Oh! what a dreadful thing!
The fire has caught her apron-string;
Her apron burns, her arms, her hair;
She burns all over, every where.

Then how the pussy-cats did mew,
What else, poor pussies, could they do?
They scream'd for help, 'twas all in vain!
So then, they said,—"we'll scream again;
Make haste, make haste, me-ow, me-o
She'll burn to death,—we told her so."

So she was burnt, with all her clothes,
And arms, and hands, and eyes and nose;
Till she had nothing more to lose
Except her little scarlet shoes;
And nothing else but these was found
Among her ashes on the ground.

And when the good cats sat beside
The smoking ashes, how they cried!
"Me-ow, me-oo, me-ow, me-oo
What will Mammà and Nursy do?"
Their tears ran down their cheeks so fast,
They made a little pond at last.

**26 Heinrich Hoffman**. *The English Struwwelpeter, or Pretty stories and funny pictures for little children.* Fourth edition. Leipsic: F. Volckmar, [1848]
[11645.f.42]
'Harriet & the matches': the little heap of ashes, the unburnt slippers and weeping pussy cats tell her fate.

Sulphur matches, on sale since 1829 and at first hailed as an emancipation for women (it made a constant watch over the hearth unnecessary), were now seen as a potential danger in children's hands. In 1842 a fire had reduced a large part of Hamburg to ashes.

I. SHOCK-HEADED PETER.

Just look at him! There he stands,
With his nasty hair and hands.
See! his nails are never cut;
They are grim'd as black as soot;
And the sloven, I declare,
Never once has comb'd his hair;
Any thing to me is sweeter
Than to see Shock-headed Peter.

(2)

**27** **Heinrich Hoffman.** *The English Struwwelpeter, or Pretty stories and funny pictures for little children ... Twelfth edition.* Leipzig: Friedrich Volckmar; London, at the Agency of the German Literary Society [1860?]
[11651.k.60]
On grounds of expense Hoffman's lithographs were in 1858 redrawn and engraved on wood and printed from electrotypes by C. Krebs-Schmitt, Frankfurt.

me that he must have been sometimes *rather tired* of his velvet, and his diamonds, and his ermine, and his grandeur.

I shouldn't like to sit in that stifling robe with such a thing as that on my head.

No doubt, the Queen must have been lovely in her youth; for though she grew rather stout in after life, yet her features, as

shown in her portrait, are certainly *pleasing*. If she was fond of flattery, scandal, cards, and fine clothes, let us deal gently

mannered, like the Queen of Hearts, the Duchess, the Hatter, and Humpty Dumpty, or grotesquely incompetent, like the White Queen and the White Knight'.

'Lewis Carroll', the Revd Charles Lutwidge Dodgson, a lecturer in mathematics at Christ Church, Oxford, used to entertain his ten-year-old friend Alice Liddell, the Dean's daughter, and her sisters with his tales, weaving fantasies around Alice's life in Victorian Oxford. At Alice's request he began in July 1862 to write down her namesake's adventures and in 1864 she received as a Christmas present the completed manuscript. *Alice's adventures under ground.* (34), written in his own hand and illustrated with his own drawings. Friends urged him to publish it, and he revised and expanded the story for printing at his own expense. Macmillans agreed to distribute the book on commission.

For publication Dodgson dropped his own illustrations and approached the *Punch* artist John Tenniel, whose animal drawings for Aesop's fables had appealed to him. Dodgson, who was paying the printer's, illustrator's and engravers' bills, gave detailed instructions about the content and placing of the illustrations. He also closely supervised Tenniel's depiction of Alice in ankle-strap shoes and pocketed apron. In a number of instances Tenniel's illustrations are modelled on Dodgson's own drawings. Tenniel retains the everyday appearance of people, animals and toys even though their actions are unreal and absurd.

**28 William Makepeace Thackeray.** *The Rose and the Ring; or, the History of Prince Giglio and Prince Bulbo ... by Mr. M.A. Titmarsh [W.M. Thackeray].* Smith, Elder & Co., 1855
[C.59.c.11]
The story, which takes as its starting point the contemporary London pantomime, was worked around the illustrations, drawn originally to amuse Thackeray's own children. Thackeray himself transferred fifty-six drawings in his manuscript on to the wood-blocks.

THE GIRL WHO WOULD NOT
LEARN TO SEW.

ow, Nelly, there's a darling girl,
  Do try and hem this handkerchief;
All little girls, as up they grow,
  Must learn to hem, and baste, and sew,
    Or they will surely come to grief.

"For you must learn to make your clothes,
  Since none but babes and dolls of wood
By other people's hands are dress'd;
  You're not a baby, that's confess'd;
    And for a doll you're far too good."

But Nelly blubbers, pouts, and cries,
  In spite of all Mamma could say;
To make a stitch she would not try,—
  Mamma exclaim'd, with many a sigh—
    "Nelly will be a doll some day!"

egardless of this dreadful doom,
  Nelly refused to learn to sew;
  Her stupid head for nothing good,
  Grew more and more like solid wood,
    Her limbs more stiff began to grow.

Her brow grew flat, her eyes grew round,
  Her arms stuck out like matches straight,
Her flesh grew hard as oak or deal,
  A stupid smile her lips reveal—
    To be a *doll* is Nelly's fate.

"So," cried Mamma, "to dress Miss Nell
  Is now the easiest thing to do:
Whene'er she wants new shoes or frocks
  We'll fetch the toyman with his box,
    To stick them on with nails and
      glue."

29 *The little minxes*. David Bogue, [1857]
[12807.f.48]
The girl who would not learn to sew is turned into a wooden doll. Text, initials
and illustration are ingeniously interwoven.

It was intended that *Alice's adventures in Wonderland* – the title eventually adopted – should be published in time for Christmas 1864, but Tenniel's delays meant a postponement until June 1865 when his last drawing was handed in. By the end of that month the Clarendon Press had printed 2,000 copies, and on 4 July a copy bound in white vellum was sent to Alice Liddell. Of these 2,000 copies about two dozen were bound and sent out as presentation copies prior to publication. Tenniel, however, was dissatisfied with the printing of his illustrations and insisted that the whole edition be withdrawn. Dodgson recalled his presentation copies, and sent them to Great Ormond Street Children's Hospital; eighteen known copies survive, and they are accorded priority as the first issue of the first edition.

The printing of a new edition was satisfactorily carried out by Richard Clay, and this was published in November 1865 – '1866' on the title-page. The remaining copies of the suppressed edition were not sold as waste-paper but sent to America with a new tipped-in title-page; this reissue was published by Appleton, New York, in 1866. In a letter to Macmillans Dodgson considered that they 'will do very well for the Americans who ought not to be very particular as to quality, as they insist on having books for very cheap'.

Here is Thoth, the inky boy,
Slinging ink his greatest joy.

If the        barber shows his shears
Then        his face is washed in tears;
And, as he were led to slaughter,
At the very sight of water
He begins to roar and bellow.
Fie! the dirty, ugly fellow!
But the gods of judgment saw
How the foul one broke their law,

Him, of purity the hater,
Named they ever Struwwelpeter;

He shall be what he hath been,
Nothing now can wash him clean!

**30** *The Egyptian Struwwelpeter*. H. Grevel, 1899
[12315.k.21]
'Here is Thoth, the inky boy
Slinging ink his greatest joy.'

**31 Richard Doyle.** *The Story of Jack and the giants. Illustrated with thirty-five drawings by Richard Doyle. Engraved by G. & E. Dalziel.* Cundall & Addey, 1851
[12430.g.3]
'The double-headed Welshman'. Doyle's hand-coloured wood engravings, commissioned by the Dalziels, illustrate legends about West Country giants of terrifying stature and habits. In one of them, cattle were substituted (at the publishers' insistence) for human victims hanging from the giant's belt.

In 1928 the original manuscript was sold to the American collector, A. S. W. Rosenbach. When it came on the market again in 1948 it was purchased (for $50,000) by a group of American wellwishers and presented to the British Museum as an expression of gratitude for Britain's defence of freedom during the Second World War. The manuscript is usually on exhibition in the British Library's galleries.

The British copyright in *Alice in Wonderland* expired in 1907 and eight editions with new illustrations appeared in the autumn of that year:

'Enchanting Alice', Black-and-White
Has made your deeds perennial,
And naught save "Chaos and old Night"
Can part you now from Tenniel'

wrote Austin Dobson in the verses with which he introduced Tenniel's new rival, Arthur Rackham (36). In Rackham's illustrations – in colour – the backgrounds of gnarled wood and tangled undergrowth sometimes overshadow the characters; but his Alice is a real girl, whereas Tenniel had made her somewhat doll-like, not very different from the cards and chess-pieces.

**33** **William McConnell.** *The laughable looking glass for little folks. Second series by Newman (one of the writers in Punch) and Hain Friswell.*
Dean & Son [1857]
[11648.f.27]
McConnell was an artist with *Punch* and other journals.

## THE ILL-NATURED, OR SELFISH BOY.

**32 Charles H. Bennett.** Darcy W. Thompson: *Fun and earnest, or Rhymes with reason.* Griffith & Farran, 1865

[11649.aa.10]

Bennett was an artist with *Punch*.

THIS IS THE
MAIDEN ALL FORLORN
THAT MILKED
The COW with the CRUMPLED
HORN
That tossed the DOG
That worried the CAT
That killed the RAT
That ate the MALT
That lay in the HOUSE
That JACK BUILT

**34 Lewis Carroll.** *Alice's adventures under ground.* [1863]
[Add.MS.46 700,f.20]
'She went on growing and growing, and very soon had to kneel down on the floor: in another minute there was not even room for this, and she tried the effect of lying down with one elbow against the door.' Of the thirty-seven drawings in the manuscript fourteen are full-page, each of these is opposite the relevant text, though most are, awkwardly, sideways.

**35 Henry George Hine.** *The Remarkable history of the House that Jack built. Splendidly illustrated and magnificently illuminated by the son of a genius. Drawn on Stone by H.G. Hine* [i.e. lithographs.]
Grant & Griffith, successors to Newbery & Harris, St. Paul's Churchyard [1854?]
[506.aa.29]
Henry George Hine, an artist with *Punch* (1841-44) and marine painter, here draws in a childishly naïve style.

**36 Arthur Rackham.** Lewis Carroll: *Alice's adventures in Wonderland.* London: William Heinemann; New York: Doubleday, Page, 1907
[K.T.C. 105.b.1]

**37 Sir John Tenniel.** Lewis Carroll: *Alice's adventures in Wonderland*. Macmillan & Co., 1865
[C.59.g.32]
'Her eyes immediately met those of a caterpillar'. Tenniel's illustrations were printed from electrotypes of the engraved woodblocks.

**38 Sir John Tenniel.** Lewis Carroll: *Alice's adventures in Wonderland*. Macmillan, 1865
[C.59.g.32]
The Mad Hatter's tea-party.

**39 Catherine Sinclair** *The picture letter*. Edinburgh: James Wood, 1861.
[12804.i.32]
Printed in colour lithography (and advertised on the cover as 'warranted to keep the noisiest child quiet for half an hour') by N.H. McFarlane, lithographers, Edinburgh.
In these letters, modelled on the *Hieroglyphic Bibles* of the eighteenth century, Catherine Sinclair substituted tiny pictures for the key words.

Another [envelope] from [cat]herine Sinclair.

My darling [duck]

Can U come to T with me soon, and

X.qqq a short Notice, but ask for the

[carriage] or come by the [station]

to morrow, and [eye] shall be glad with all

my [heart] to see U. We shall have some cold

[sheep] and a roast [rabbit] also a [basket of fruit]

an [peach] [pie] and a [jug] of fresh Milk

from the [cow] Put on strong [shoe]

as we must sail in a [boat] and go to your

[chest of drawers] for an old [dress] that we may pick

[strawberries] visit the [beehives] and the [windmill]

# Edmund Evans and his artists

## Toy-books

Toy-books, which first appeared soon after the accession of Queen Victoria in 1837, consisted of six or eight square pages of coloured illustrations, sometimes accompanied by a short text (**22**), usually a traditional tale or rhyme. The covers were of paper, and the price was low. Colour was the important element in toy-books, whether applied by means of chromolithography or wood-blocks, or by hand.

Walter Crane, writing later of the toy-books of the mid-century, complained of their 'generally careless and unimaginative woodcuts, very casually coloured by hand, dabs of pink and emerald green being laid across faces and frocks with a somewhat careless aim'. The toy-books printed by chromolithography were 'heavily printed, oily and terrible'.

**40** *The Wonderland Quadrilles. Composed for the piano-forte by C.H.R. Marriott.* Music cover. Chromo-lithograph after Tenniel, about 1872
[h.1359/20]

**41** Mrs Sherwood: *The story of little Henry and his bearer Boosy.* Houlston & Wright, 1866
[4415.ccc.13]
Pathos and exotic local colour are used for a religious purpose in the story of the orphan Henry who, at the age of seven, converts his devoted bearer and dies in the odour of sanctity.
The colour-printed frontispiece is by Joseph Martin Kronheim.

" Here they sat down; and Henry could not but admire the beautiful prospect which was before them. On their left was the broad stream of the Ganges winding round the curved shore, till it was lost behind the *Raja mehal* hills."

Colour printing was nearly always more expensive than hand-colouring for small editions and, apart from some frontispieces, (41) not much used in books for children until the 1860s. The publishers such as Frederick Warne, Ward, Lock and George Routledge then began to issue their six-penny and shilling toy-book series in editions of tens of thousands.

## Edmund Evans

Edmund Evans, who had been apprenticed to Ebenezer Landells, a pupil of Bewick's, in 1851 set up his own engraving and printing office, which he conducted with a rare combination of technical expertise, taste and business sense until the end of the century. Evans believed that toy-books could be much improved and still sold for sixpence if printed in sufficient quantity. He filled the gaps between print-runs by initiating his own series of children's picture-books of high quality, printed in colour throughout and selling for a few pence.

## Walter Crane

Walter Crane, the son of a portrait painter, was apprenticed at the age of thirteen to William James Linton, another pupil of Bewick's, from whom he learned not engraving but the quite separate craft of drawing designs on the wood for others to engrave.

After Crane had completed his apprenticeship small jobs came his way from Linton and from Edmund Evans. In 1863 Evans commissioned three toy-books from Crane which he printed for Warne, and in 1865 the first two of Crane's books in Routledge's Sixpenny series, to which other artists and engravers had by then already contributed thirty-six items.

Crane had clear ideas about what children wanted; he later wrote in an article in *The Imprint* (1913):

'Children, like the ancient Egyptians, appear to see most things in profile, and like definite statements in design. They prefer well-defined forms and bright, frank colour. They don't want to bother about three dimensions. They can accept symbolic representations. They themselves employ drawing, like the ancient races, as a kind of picture-writing and eagerly follow a pictured story. When they can count they will check your quantities, so that the artist must be careful to deliver in . . . 'The Song of Sixpence', his tale of twenty-four blackbirds'. (42)

Crane believed that a child's imagination should be stimulated. He also regarded the illustration of books for children as a suitable task for those who wished to challenge accepted taste:

'They are attractive to designers of an imaginative tendency, for in a sober and matter-of-fact age they afford perhaps the only outlet for unrestrained flights of fancy open to the modern illustrator who likes to revolt against the despotism of facts'.

Crane continued to draw his own designs on the block until 1871, the year of his marriage and a protracted stay in Rome. By then it had become possible to photograph the key outline direct on to wood from drawings

**42 Walter Crane.** *Sing a song of sixpence* Geo. Routledge, 1866. (Sixpenny toy books)

[12806.h.99]

The figures are without backgrounds; the text, with its large blue and red initials, forms part of design. Crane here still uses crosshatching and parallel lines to suggest tonal gradations. (See page 80 for colour reproduction.)

made on card, and these he sent back by post. But apart from his not having to handle the blocks, Crane's method remained the same:

He made pencil sketches, trying out variant compositions. When satisfied, he would produce one or more full-colour finished drawings, trace the outlines and transfer them to the block (or to the card, when photography was used). Evan's engravers then cut the block. Crane received black and white proofs, which he would tint and return to Evans, who then had a block made for each colour. Even when primary colours were overprinted to give a wider range of colours, five or six separate blocks and printings would normally be required and sometimes as many as eight. Evans mixed the colours for printing with the same pigments that Crane had used in the proofs.

## The Sixpenny toy-books

With Crane and Evans the toy-book became something approaching a distinctive art-form. Crane understood the limitations of wood-engraving

The Captain
was a Duck,
With a jacket
on his back.

**43 Walter Crane.** *The Fairy Ship*. George Routledge, 1870. (Sixpenny toy books)

[12806.h.24]

In Crane's depiction of the ship manned by mice and commanded by a duck, he used red, yellow and blue and the colours obtained from superimposing them. Note Crane's monogram – a long-legged crane.

IN THE CORNER.

**44 J.G. Sowerby.** *At home. Illustrated by J.G. Sowerby. Decorated by Thomas Crane.* London, Belfast: Marcus Ward & Co. [1881]

[12805.k.41]

Walter Crane's brother Thomas was art director of Marcus Ward, the firm that had cornered the greetings card market in 1870 when the Franco-Prussian war prevented imports from the Continent. He began to publish children's books in 1873. *At Home* records the home life of children who live in a 'Queen Anne' house.

in colour and made the most of this apparently inflexible graphic method. He took the double-page spread as the visual unit. Text and illustration were planned together, and Crane sometimes wrote the text out himself. His hand-drawn letters were graceful but unvaried; but his decorative motifs, many of them floral, were endlessly inventive.

In some toy-books full-page pictures alternated with pages of text, but in those by Crane text and picture usually appear on the same page, and to prevent 'see-through' from over-inking, only one side of the sheet was printed. The blank versos which interrupt the story did not carry text – this was inscribed on tablets within the illustrations.

The whole story had to be contained within the eight-leaf structure. While he sometimes employed panel-by-panel narrative Crane often abandoned a linear progression of incidents taking place within the same pictorial space and used an emphatic feature in one drawing to introduce the next, with sudden shifts of point of view and perspective. He also followed the medieval convention of depicting in one illustration the same characters at different points of time.

Crane describes the decisive influence of Japanese prints on his work: 'Their treatment in definite black outline and flat, brilliant as well as delicate colours, struck me at once and I endeavoured to apply these methods to the modern fanciful and humorous subjects of children's toy-books.' In the Sixpenny toy-books his figures float in a shallow space. Their limbs, sometimes cut off at the knee or the elbow by the frame, lack the solidity suggested by modelling, and their faces have no individuality. While there is little sense of depth or movement in these ingenious de-signs, they nevertheless show a complete control of elaborate pattern.

## Crane and the 'Aesthetic' Movement

As well as being an illustrator, Crane was a designer of textiles, furniture, gesso work, wallpapers, stained glass and ceramic tiles. He also painted murals and panels, and in his toy-books we find fashionable 'aesthetic' interiors, inhabited by graceful figures in richly patterned garments:

'I was accustomed to introduce into the children's books decorative details that interested me at the time and was concerned with in other work . . . I believe that, in early days, occasionally architects even used some of the picture-books to show their clients the kind of thing they ought to have in their houses.'

Crane became a leading figure in the Arts and Crafts movement and received commissions for furnishings modelled on those in his toy-books. *The Absurd ABC* (48) for example, anticipates his nursery wall-paper designs for Messrs Jeffrey & Co.

The 'Aesthetic' movement encouraged the use of light, clear colours, especially green and yellow, and favoured a vaguely 'Queen Anne' style in architecture and furniture. This too is noticeable in the children's picture-books printed by Evans, and in particular in those by Crane.

They not only show approved 'aesthetic' accessories – decorated tiles, blue and white china, lightweight chairs, sun-flowers, peacock feathers, bay windows with leaded lights and roundels of stained glass – but follow the same recipe as the 'Queen Anne' architects: a free selection of 17th- and 18th-century elements mixed with a little of almost everything else (especially Japanese details) to produce a highly original result.

## Crane's later work

By 1875 Crane had done twenty-nine Sixpenny toy-books for Routledge, and eight Shilling toy-books. He sold his drawings direct to the publishers. While he was in Italy Routledges issued, without his knowledge, an omnibus 'Walter Crane's Picture Book'. Crane complained that although this volume, featured his name on previously anonymous work it was nevertheless 'far from being what I should have approved in its general format'. He received no money for these re-issues and when he asked for a higher fee, 'or at least a small royalty', this was refused, and another artist was sought to replace Crane. Randolph Caldecott was approached by Evans about a new Shilling toy-book Series, and Caldecott was able to secure a royalty for his work.

In 1877 the earlier partnership tried a new format in Crane's *The Baby's opera* (45), a volume of illustrated songs for children, priced at 5s. Crane explained:

**45 Walter Crane.** Lucy Crane: *The Baby's opera. A book of old rhymes in new dresses ... The music by the earliest masters.* George Routledge [1877]
[B.204]
'At first the trade shook its head,' wrote Crane: 'A five-shilling book not decently bound in cloth and without any gold on it was an unheard of thing ... Some said "this will never do", but it did. The first edition of ten thousand copies was soon exhausted'. The cover is both inviting and allusive; see, for example, the eloping 'willow pattern' Dish and Spoon.

**46** (*Overleaf*): **Walter Crane**. *Ali Baba and the forty thieves*, G. Routledge, 1873
[12806.f.1(2.)]

then went to bed; and Morgiana happening to need oil, went to help herself out of the jars of the guest; she found, instead of oil, a man in every jar but one. Determined that they should not escape, and heating a quantity of oil, she poured some into each jar, killing the robber within. So when the captain gave the signal to his men, none of them appeared, and going to the jars he found them all dead; so he went his way full of rage and despair, and returned to the cave, and there formed a project of revenge. Next day he went into the town, and hiring a warehouse, which he furnished with rich goods, became acquainted with

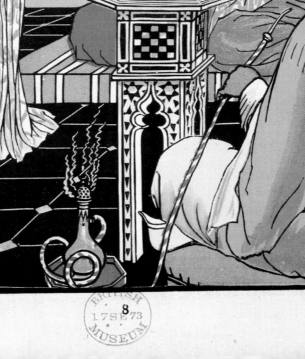

Ali Baba's son, who one day invited him to his father's house. On hearing that the new guest would eat no salt with his meat, Morgiana's suspicions were aroused, and she recognised him as the captain of the robbers. After dinner she undertook to perform a dance before the company, and at the end of it pointed a dagger at the captain, and then plunged it into his heart. Ali Baba was very much shocked, until Morgiana explained the reasons for her conduct; he then gave her to his son in marriage, and they lived in great prosperity and happiness ever after.

8

'About 1874 or 1875, I think I designed some sets of six and eight-inch fireplace tiles for Messrs Maw & Co... The treatment did not differ much from the treatment of similar subjects in full pages of *The Baby's Opera* – in fact, I rather think that the square form, size and treatment of the six-inch tiles really suggested the adoption of the same size and treatment for the book, which must have been planned very shortly afterwards'.

'My *Baby's Opera*... proved so successful that the publishers wanted on to follow it up immediately by another. Being engaged in other work I did not see my way to this; but the publishers were equal to the emergency, for I was rather startled about Christmas to see Kate Greenaway's first book, *Under the Window* announced by them as "companion volume to *The Baby's Opera*". To this I naturally objected as misleading, and the advertisement was withdrawn'.

Crane's *Baby's Bouquet*, a true companion, was nevertheless ready for Christmas 1878. Both Crane's new books combined pictures, words and music on the same page. The colours were soft, and there was proliferation of children (almost completely absent in Crane's earlier picture-books) in high-waisted dresses, aprons, bonnets or knee-breeches, rather like those of Kate Greenaway.

## Randolph Caldecott

When Routledges declined to pay Crane royalties, and he ceased work on their Shilling Picture Books, Evans needed a new artist. In his *Reminiscences* he recorded:

'I thought Randolph Caldecott would be just the man to do some Shilling Toybooks... so I appointed a meeting with him in his lodgings in Great Russell Street'. [Caldecott] 'feeling sure of his own powers... wished to share in the speculation – said he would make the drawings – if they sold and paid, he would be paid, but was content to bear the loss if they did not sell'.

Evans agreed to take the risks of engraving all the blocks needed for Caldecott's colouring:

'the key block in *dark brown*, then a *flesh tint*, for the faces, hands and wherever it would bring other colours as nearly as possible to his painted copy, a *red*, a *blue*, a *yellow* and a *grey*. I was to supply the paper and print 10,000 copies... Shilling Toybooks at that time generally had blank pages at the back of the pictures. I proposed to have no blanks at all.' [The use of heavier paper made this possible.]

Caldecott's sketches, in combination with full-page colour illustrations, were printed with the text in brown ink, which would, he believed, 'stand any number of deep assaults' of superimposed colour.

Until he was twenty-five, Caldecott had worked as a bank-clerk in Whitchurch, Shropshire, where he lived in a farm-house and in his spare time went fishing and shooting. He used to attend hunts, steeplechases, markets and cattle-fairs, storing country sights and people in his sketch-book and his memory.

**47 Ernest Griset**. *The Favorite Album of Fun and Fancy with illustrations by Ernest Griset and others*. London, Paris & New York: Cassell, Petter, Galpin & Co. [1880]

[12809.n.26]

Griset, born in France in 1844, gained early recognition in London as a caricaturist working for *Punch*. Like his fellow countryman Grandville, Griset was expert in expressing human emotions through his naturalistically drawn animals, but without Grandville's savagely satirical intent; and like Edward Lear, he lived near the London Zoo where he found convenient models.

Caldecott's illustrations in his first Shilling Picture Books, *John Gilpin* (51) and *The House that Jack built* have Crane's strong outlines and areas of colour but without his heavy borders. The racy, spontaneous character of his own Washington Irving illustrations (1876) prevailed. *The Times* reviewer wrote: 'In a few strokes dashed off apparently at random, he can portray a scene or incident to the full as correctly and completely, and far more lucidly than Mr Crane in his later and far more elaborate style'.

Caldecott studied 'the art of leaving out as a science', remembering, as he used to say, that 'the fewer the lines the less error committed'. He handled space with complete assurance to convey a sense of delight in movement and energy.

He did not merely transpose the words of a text into visual equivalents but amplified and explained a story. Thus 'Sing a song for sixpence' is

**48** (*Overleaf*): **Walter Crane**. *The Absurd A.B.C.* George Routledge & Sons, [1874] (Walter Crane's Toy Books. New Series)

[12806.f.1(5.)]

Crane used black as a colour as well as for outlines. His designs here make a light-hearted allusion to the vase-painting of the ancient world.

# KLM

N for t

Were

th

L for Little man, gun and
bullets complete,
Who shot the poor duck, and
was proud of the feat.

K for calm Kitty, at dinner
who sat,
While all the good folks
watched the dog & the cat.

ous children
who
much for
r in Shoe.

O the Old person that
cobwebs did spy,
And went up to sweep 'em
Oh ever so high !

P for the Pie made of
blackbirds to sing,
A song fit for supper
a dish for a king.

M for Miss Muffet, with
that horrid spider,
st dropped into tea and
a chat beside her.

"Since you have caught cold," Miss MOUSEY said,

  *Heigho, says* ROWLEY!

"I'll sing you a song that I have just made."

  *With a rowley-powley, gammon and spinach,*

  *Heigho, says* ANTHONY ROWLEY!

both updated and demythologized, and the frog who would a-wooing go asks the rat to accompany him to Miss Mouse's house (**49**) because he is too shy to go alone.

From 1878 until his early death in 1886 Caldecott prepared two picture-books a year for the Christmas trade. They seem to be the work of a boisterous, no-nonsense sort of horseman, but he was very much the aesthete and a practising craftsman. (He carved the capitals in Lord Leighton's Arab Hall in Melbury Road, Kensington, where Crane designed the mosaics.) There is less 'Queen Anne' *bric à brac* than in Crane's toy-books, but where it appears it is treated with easy playfulness. Caldecott, in William Feaver's words, gives us 'a vision of a nut-brown, pale pea-green, hunting-pink Old England – Rowlandson's England, tidied, mellowed, with smiles instead of leers'.

## Kate Greenaway

As an escape from the squalor and ugliness of Victorian cities the artists and aesthetes of the Arts and Crafts movement tried to re-create a 'Never-never' land of rural simplicity and promoted a cult of the innocence and charm of childhood. Middle-class parents were ready for Kate Greenaway's presentation of the everyday life of children in idyllic pre-industrial surroundings, and her books found immediate popularity with reviewers and public.

Kate Greenaway had been working for some years as an illustrator, especially of Christmas cards, when her father, a wood-engraver, showed Edmund Evans a notebook of her drawings and verses. Evans offered to buy it outright, and undertook to print the work of this little-known artist in an edition of 20,000 copies. The sales of *Under the Window* (1878) (**54**) confirmed Evans' judgement and began a steady flow of Kate Greenaway's picture-books, story-books and almanacs.

When *Under the Window* was advertised as a companion volume to *The Baby's Opera*, Walter Crane maintained that Kate Greenaway's work was merely a 'pretty book of nursery rhymes, with illustrations treated, as far as the outline and flat tint method went, in a similar way to mine, but less formal, without the decorative borders, without the music and of quite a different size'. Children were only one of Crane's subjects, while Kate Greenaway drew almost nothing else.

Unlike Crane's backgrounds, the village streets of 'Queen Anne' cottages and old-fashioned gardens in which her children play never fill the frame or page. Space flows around both illustrations and printed text with a refreshingly light effect. Few of her books, apart from *The Queen of the Pirate Isle* (**front cover**) illustrate a sustained narrative.

Kate Greenaway drew from models wearing costumes she made herself, copied largely but not exclusively from the high-waisted dresses and jackets, buttoned breeches and smocks of the late eighteenth century. They also wore mob-caps (early eighteenth-century) and the big straw hats, muffs and bonnets of her own day. While Crane later conceded that her little girls, prim gardens and old-world atmosphere 'captivated the

**51 Randolph Caldecott.** *John Gilpin.* George Routledge & Sons (1878)
(Randolph Caldecott's Picture Books)
[12805.k.61(1.)]

**52 Kate Greenaway.** *A, Apple pie. By K.G.* George Routledge [1886]
[12806.u.12]
Ruskin called Kate Greenaway's drawings of feet 'paddles or flappers'. 'You should go to some watering place in August', he urged her, 'with fine sands – and draw no end of bare feet'.

**53 Kate Greenaway.** *Marigold garden.* G. Routledge & Sons [1885]
[12810.dd.39]
There may be an element of gentle self-parody in 'A genteel family'.

## A GENTEEL FAMILY.

SOME children are so naughty,
　And some are very good ;
But the Genteel Family
　Did always what it should.

They put on gloves when they went out,
　And ran not in the street ;
And on wet days not one of them
　Had ever muddy feet.

KG

INDEED it is true, it is perfectly true;
  Believe me, indeed, I am playing no tricks;
An old man and his dog bide up there in the moon,
  And he's cross as a bundle of sticks.

**54** **Kate Greenaway.** *Under the window. Pictures and rhymes by K.G.*
Engraved and printed by E. Evans. G. Routledge & Sons, [1879]
[12805.1.17]
Kate Greenaway's preparatory drawings and manuscript survive and show that
some of the verses were entirely rewritten before publication. The pictures
came first and she then fitted her own words to them. In the table of contents
each item is ingeniously listed by a tiny reduced facsimile of the corresponding
page.

**55** **Florence Upton.** *The adventures of two Dutch dolls and a Golliwogg,*
Longmans & Co. [1895]

[12809.t.1]

Florence Upton, an English girl brought up in New York, when on a visit to
England with her mother in 1893 made some sketches using wooden dolls as
models (Sarah Jane and Peggy, dressed here in the Stars and Stripes), but for a
good story she still needed a hero. Her grandmother came to light with a black
doll, the favourite of Florence's American childhood, for whom Florence
invented the name 'Golliwogg' and her mother wrote the verses. Thirteen
Golliwogg books, including the hand-drawn text were lithographed by the
Niagara Lithographic Co., Buffalo, N.Y.

During the First World War Florence Upton put her Dutch dolls and
Golliwogg up for auction, together with her manuscripts and drawings, to raise
money for an ambulance (called Golliwogg). The purchasers presented them to
the British Prime Minister's country house at Chequers, where they remain to
this day.

public in a remarkable way', he meekly added; 'May I confess that (for me at least) ... she overdid the big bonnet rather, and at one time her little people were almost lost in their clothes?'

Kate Greenaway insisted on the return of her drawings after printing. When there were no royalties to be paid on the text (she often wrote her own) she received a third or half the profits. Her earnings, which averaged £2,000 for each of her books, enabled her to support her parents who lived with her in her 'Queen Anne' house (by Norman Shaw) in Frognal, Hampstead.

## Beatrix Potter

Among the pictures purchased by Beatrix Potter's father, a wealthy non-practising barrister, were thirty of Caldecott's sketches, including those for *A frog he would a woo-ing go* and a set of the *Three Jovial Huntsmen*. Beatrix Potter herself became an accomplished artist, especially in depicting animals, and in her mid-thirties entertained the children of her former governess with picture-letters relating the supposed adventures of her own pets. Out of one of these letters grew *The tale of Peter Rabbit*. Beatrix Potter was encouraged to offer the manuscript to half-a-dozen publishers, including Frederick Warne, before publishing it at her own expense, on 16 December 1901. In this privately printed edition her forty-two pen-and-ink sketches were reproduced in black and white.

On the same day Warne wrote to her accepting *Peter Rabbit*, on condition that she prepare illustrations in colour, to be reduced in number to thirty, plus a frontispiece. At Warne's suggestion some of the text was deleted and later transferred to *The Tale of Benjamin Bunny* (1904). It was, however, Beatrix Potter's own idea that her illustrations should be reproduced by the recently developed three-colour process, and she was closely involved in every stage of production of *Peter Rabbit* The first commercial edition eventually appeared in October 1902, in 6,000 copies, printed by Edmund Evans.

The elements of Beatrix Potter's mildly cautionary tales are those of traditional stories and rhymes, treated with varying degrees of irony and enhanced by the consistent elegance of her language. Her masterpieces of concise narrative not only avoid baby-talk but actively enlarge a very young reader's vocabulary. They are inseparable, too, from her illustrations. While Kate Greenaway, another Londoner, depicted an idealized countryside which existed mainly in her own imagination, Beatrix Potter's drawings are minutely specific, and in many instances modelled on her own animals, and on rooms and objects in her cottage in the Lake Country. ('I spent a very wet hour *inside* the pig-sty drawing the pig').

Beatrix Potter admitted the influence of the Pre-Raphaelites in her meticulous handling of natural detail, and this affectionate precision conveys the essence of animal-nature in her drawn creatures, despite their clothes (usually shed in the course of the story), their houses and furniture. Millais once said to her: 'Plenty of people can draw but you have observation'.

# Matilda,

*Who told Lies, and was Burned to Death.*

Matilda told such Dreadful Lies,

It made one Gasp and Stretch one's Eyes;

Her Aunt, who, from her Earliest Youth,

Had kept a Strict Regard for Truth,

**56 Lord Basil Blackwood.** Hilaire Belloc. *The bad child's book of beasts, together with Cautionary tales.* London: Duckworth, 1896

[12802.c.45]

'Matilda, growing tired of play,

And finding she was left alone,

Went tiptoe to the Telephone

And summoned the Immediate Aid,

Of London's Noble Fire-Brigade'.

'B.T.B.''s witty draughtsmanship match perfectly Belloc's worldly parodies of the cautionary tale.

'NOW, my dears,' said old Mrs. Rabbit one morning, 'you may go into the fields or down the lane, but don't go into Mr. McGregor's garden: your Father had an accident there; he was put in a pie by Mrs. McGregor.'

BUT Flopsy, Mopsy, and Cotton-tail had bread and milk and blackberries for supper.

**57 Beatrix Potter.** *The Tale of Peter Rabbit. By Beatrix Potter.* London & New York: Frederick Warne, 1902
[Cup.402.a.4]

# Gift books

In the 1860s, popular graphic artists had been commissioned to design *de luxe* gift-books intended for the drawing-room rather than the nursery, although cheap trade editions of them were also on sale. During the first two decades of this century, technical innovations again encouraged the production of lavishly decorated gift-books, in gilt blocked bindings with ornamental head-bands and end-papers, and sometimes a coloured illustration mounted on the upper cover. The colour plates were reproduced by the new three-colour process, and had to be printed on glossy art-paper, tipped on to cartridge mounts and protected with tissue paper. Among the artists who worked on gift-books were the Robinson brothers, Arthur Rackham and Edmund Dulac.

## Charles Robinson

After the success of *Treasure Island*, Robert Louis Stevenson thought, rightly, that he could improve on Mrs Sale Barker's verses in Kate Greenaway's *Birthday book for children*, (1880). In Stevenson's *Child's Garden of Verses* (1885), the emotions of childhood are simply and convincingly expressed. For the edition published by The Bodley Head in 1896, John Lane chose a young illustrator, Charles Robinson, who provided not only *art nouveau* drawings of unusual charm but hand-lettered titles and sensitively placed (and spaced) head and tail-pieces (58). *A Child's Garden of Verses* made Robinson's reputation, and he went on to illustrate well over a hundred books, many of them for children.

Robinson had served his apprenticeship as a lithographer, but was one of the first illustrators to have all his work reproduced by line- and half-tone blocks. Following Walter Crane's precept and practice, he designed each book as a whole. He usually prepared sketches to show publishers his proposals for page layout – often counter-balanced and intertwining areas of text and illustration – as well as for bindings, end-papers and vignettes.

Charles Robinson and his brothers, Thomas and William Heath Robinson, came of a family who had for two generations worked as illustrators and engravers. Though it was Charles who first won acclaim,

**58 Charles Robinson.**
Robert Louis Stevenson:
*A child's garden of verses.*
John Lane, 1896
[K.T.C.33.a.4]

PICTURE BOOKS IN WINTER.

Heath Robinson's name has since passed into the language to describe the improvised and futile contraptions he devised for his humorous drawings in the weekly papers of the 1920s.

## William Heath Robinson

In 1897 William Heath Robinson shared with his two brothers a commission to illustrate an edition of Hans Christian Andersen's tales. Heath Robinson, like Aubrey Beardsley, drew in a clear sinuous line and was expert in the deployment of white space with masses of black. This gives even his most detailed designs a sense of rhythm and integration. In *Uncle Lubin* (1902) the story as well as the drawings are from his pen; and we find the first suggestions of his comically complicated devices. Heath Robinson's next original children's book was *Bill the Minder* (1912) **(59)**, a series of stories about the adventures of a professional babysitter. His own children usually sat for the preliminary studies but not for the worked-up drawings. For really eccentric poses Heath Robinson would (with the aid of a mirror) act as his own model.

## Arthur Rackham

Arthur Rackham was a fine draughtsman in black and white work **(63, 64)**, but it was his watercolours for *Alice in Wonderland* (1907) **(36)** that brought him lasting fame.

In his use of the half-tone colour-block to create images of mystery and timelessness Rackham avoided a vividly coloured naturalism. In the depiction of craggy mountains and gloomy woods, peopled by witches, goblins and grotesque old men Rackham is unequalled. To integrate his misty greys, faded blues and dark greens with the strong black strokes of his initial brush drawing he applied a final sepia wash.

Rackham believed in the 'stimulating and educative power of imaginative, fantastic, and playful pictures and writings for children'. He also insisted that 'nothing less than the best that can be had (and it can hardly be cheap) is good enough for those early impressionable years when standards are formed for life'.

Rackham's illustrations can be both reassuring and disquieting to the eye of childhood. Lord Clark recalled: 'I sometimes caught sight of his drawings before I was on my guard and they stamped on my imagination images of terror that troubled me for years'. But the subdued autumn tints of gnarled trees and weathered buildings are sometimes a foil for ivory-skinned maidens and good-humoured gnomes.

Rackham made his drawings twice the size in which they were to be reproduced, and once his reputation enabled him to sell the originals, he tended to work even larger. When fantasy required a tangible basis, his family – and the trees in his garden – served him as models.

## Edmund Dulac

Edmund Dulac studied law and then art in his native France, before his watercolours for *Stories from the Arabian Nights* (1907) **(65)** established

**59 William Heath Robinson.** *Bill the Minder. Written & illustrated by W. Heath Robinson.* London: Constable, 1912
[Tab.444.d.12]
In November 1910 Heath Robinson signed a contract with Constable for a book of sixteen stories, with sixteen colour plates and 120 in black and white, to be delivered by December 1911, for which he received £300.

# THE DOCTOR

**60 Grant Richards's Children's Annual, 1904**

[P.P.6753.daa]

An illustration is mounted on the cloth binding, in which motifs from nursery
rhymes appear in roundels.

**61 Henriette Willebeek Le Mair**. R.H. Elkin: *The Children's Corner* ...
Illustrations by H. Willebeek Le Mair. Philadelphia: David McKay; London:
Augener, 1914
[1873.d.5]
'Greedy'
In 1904 Henriette Willebeek Le Mair, the daughter of a rich Dutch merchant,
published her first book in France. She, like E. Boyd Smith (**67**), was
influenced by the pastel colours and flowing line of Boutet de Monvel.
She made countless preliminary sketches, and it is said that she sometimes
doused the children who were her models with water to make their clothes cling
to their bodies, so that she could observe their forms and movements more
closely. Her portrayal of carefree children, absorbed in a world of toys and
make-believe, avoids the vacuous sentimentality of the verses.

## The Motor Car Dumpy Book.

THIS is the old gentleman who used to walk in front of steam-driven carriages on the King's highway. He carried in his hand a red flag which he waved.

This is the policeman you will see all along the road. He has a watch in his hand, so that if you want to know the time you can ask him.

This is the magistrate who fines you £20 if you have been driving too fast. It is best not to drive too fast.

**62 J.R. Monsell.** T.W.H. Crosland: *The motor car Dumpy book . . . illustrated in colours by J.R. Monsell.* Grant Richards, 1904
[012806.de.34/32]
The Automobile Association was founded in 1905 as a motoring lobby, provoked by the rigorous enforcement of a speed-limit recently raised from 14 m.p.h. to 20 m.p.h. Monsell, an Irish illustrator, was a contributor to children's periodicals and to Arthur Mee's *Children's Encyclopaedia.*

**63 Arthur Rackham.** *Aesop's fables. A new translation by V.S. Vernon Jones... Illustrations by Arthur Rackham.* London: William Heinemann. New York: Doubleday Page, 1912
[12304.dd.30]

**64 Arthur Rackham.** *Mother Goose. The old nursery rhymes.* William Heinemann, 1913
[11646.h.32]
After the success of his *Alice* illustrations Rackham was more or less free to choose his texts. The verses in *Mother Goose* are his selection.

PUSSY-CAT, pussy-cat, where have you been?
I've been up to London to look at the queen.
Pussy-cat, pussy-cat, what did you there?
I frighten'd a little mouse under the chair.

**65 Edmund Dulac.** *Stories from the Arabian Nights. Retold by Laurence Housman.* With drawings by Edmund Dulac. Hodder & Stoughton, 1907
[Tab.435.c.1]
'Ali Baba': Cassim and his wife.

**66 Sir William Nicholson.** Margery Williams: *The velveteen rabbit, or how toys become real.* Heinemann, 1922
[12801.d.49]
Nicholson, a painter of landscapes, portraits and still life, was also well-known for the bold and innovative 'Beggarstaff' posters he had helped produce in the 1890s. For his illustrated albums, which included two for children, *An alphabet* (1899) and *The square book of animals* (1900), Nicholson cut his designs in masses of black directly on to the wood, and trade editions were printed by lithography. Nicholson here drew colour lithographs on the stone, from which transfers were taken and the book was printed, not entirely to his satisfaction, from zinc plates in the USA. Nicholson was charmed by the tale of a worn out toy that, like Pinocchio, came alive – the reverse of 'The girl who would not learn to sew' (**29**).

**67 E. Boyd Smith.** *The Story of Noah's Ark. Told and pictured by E. Boyd Smith*. London: Archibald Constable; Boston & New York: Houghton Miffin, 1905, Printed at the Riverside Press.

[1876.a.64]

'Life at sea'.

The American illustrator E. Boyd Smith spent his formative years working in France. Boyd Smith, like Boutet de Monvel, allowed little shadow and used thin, soft colours and a fluent unaccented line.

him as a highly successful illustrator in England. They were commissioned by Ernest Brown of the Leicester Galleries, whose sponsorship of Arthur Rackham had encouraged the young Dulac to show Brown some of his drawings. The Galleries agreed to find a publisher for a series of *Arabian Nights* illustrations and to pay Dulac a fee outright for his watercolours and the copyright. As it happened, Hodder & Stoughton had already asked Lawrence Housman to provide the text for an edition of the *Arabian Nights*, and they saw how suitable Dulac's work was for colour reproduction. Brown then guaranteed Dulac work on one book a year, on subjects to be chosen jointly with the publishers. By this agreement the Leicester Galleries commissioned and exhibited Dulac's designs and 'sub-let' them as art-work, thus sparing him the day-to-day problems of production.

Rackham obtained subtle effects using a minimum of tinting; but Dulac made a fuller use of the new three-colour process in books, and even turned its limitations to good account, for example, in his black pen-strokes, which could then be reproduced only from the three overlaid impressions of colour as a soft, blurred, and not truly black line.

Dulac worked from a careful pencil foundation, overlaid by water-colour, gouache or body colour. Even his most stylized subjects are grounded in accurate observation and sound anatomy. In compostion, too, Dulac was a meticulous craftsman, first making his rough sketches of figures on tracing paper which he then cut up, reversed and rearranged to obtain a tighter or more balanced effect.

Dulac raised to perfection a graphic style remote from the everyday world, consciously reminiscent of Persian and Indian book illumination, and looking forward to the *art déco* of the 1920s. He excelled in nocturnal or shadowy scenes where figures and forms, lit by pin-points of light, stand out against deep blue or violet backgrounds. Nothing, however, is am-biguous or flesh-creeping. Dulac's bejewelled monsters and giants pose no real threat to his silk-clad princesses and bazaar urchins.

**68 Harry Clarke.** *Fairy Tales by Hans Christian Andersen. Illustrated by Harry Clarke.*
*London:* G.G. Harrap [1917].

[K.T.C.102.a.15]

Harry Clarke, at the age of twenty-four, showed some of his drawings to George Harrap,
who decided on the strength of what he saw 'to commit my firm to a major book of the
character that is usually entrusted only to artists who have "arrived"'.

In these sinister and even disturbing illustrations Beardsley's influence is unmistakable.
Clarke, a designer of stained glass, achieves a richly patterned effect through decorative
detail. As in some of Gustav Klimt's paintings, background and costume merge so that
only faces and hands indicate the presence of people.

# Suggestions for further reading

## General

Gerald Gottlieb *Early children's books and their illustration.* Pierpont Morgan Library: Oxford University Press, 1975.

Margaret Crawford Maloney (ed.) *English illustrated books for children. A descriptive companion to a selection from the Osborne Collection ... Toronto Public Library.* The Bodley Head, 1981.

F.J. Harvey Darton *Children's books in England. Five centuries of social life. Third edition revised by Brian Alderson.* Cambridge University Press, 1983.

Lewis Carroll *Alice's adventures under ground.* (A facsimile edition.) Pavilion Books, 1985.

Brian Alderson *Sing a Song for Sixpence. The English Picture Book Tradition and Randolph Caldecott.* Cambridge University Press in association with the British Library, 1986.

## Anthologies

*Flowers of Delight culled by Leonard de Vries from the Osborne Collection of Early Children's Books ... 1765-1830.* Dennis Dobson, 1965.

*Little Wide-awake. An anthology from Victorian children's books and periodicals in the collection of Anne and Fernand G. Renier. Selected by Leonard de Vries.* Arthur Barker, 1967.

*A nursery companion. Provided by Iona and Peter Opie.* (With introduction and notes.) Oxford University Press, 1980.

## Technical

Ruari McLean *Victorian Book Design and colour printing.* (Second edition, enlarged and revised.) London: Faber & Faber, 1972.

Geoffrey Wakeman *Victorian book illustration. The technical revolution.* Newton Abbot: David & Charles, 1973.

Eric de Maré *The Victorian woodblock illustrators.* Gordon Fraser, 1980.